YOU CAN SPELL 3

WALTER T. PETTY and GUS P. PLESSAS

1968

ALLYN AND BACON, INC.

BOSTON · ROCKLEIGH, N. J. · ATLANTA · DALLAS · BELMONT, CAL.

ILLUSTRATED BY JERRY PINKNEY

CONTENTS

YOUR STUDY STEPS

Follow these five steps every time you study a word.

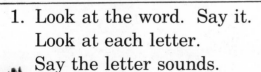

1. Look at the word. Say it.
   Look at each letter.
   Say the letter sounds.

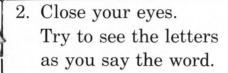

2. Close your eyes.
   Try to see the letters
   as you say the word.

3. Check to see if you
   spelled the word right.
   If not, go back to Step 1.

4. Cover the word and write it.
   Check to see if it is right.
   If not, go back to Step 1.

5. Write the word again.
   Check to see if it is right.
   If not, go back to Step 1.

YOUR SPELLING PLAN

1. Your Words

- Look at your spelling words. Say each one softly.

- Take the pretest. Check your test paper.

- Make your study list.

- Write your spelling words. Look at each letter.

- Read the story. Do what the book says.

- Study your spelling words. Follow the study steps.

2. Know About Your Words

- Do Know About Your Words.

- Study your spelling words.

- If you have extra time, do Something Extra.

3. Try Your Words

- Take the trial test. Listen carefully.

- After the test, check your words.

- Make a list of the words you missed for review.

- Study the words you missed. Follow the study steps.

4. Understand Your Words

- Do Understand Your Words.

- Study the words you missed on the trial test.

- If you have extra time, do Something Extra.

5. Remember Your Words

- Take the final test. Check your test.

- Mark your score on your Progress Chart.

YOUR REVIEW PLAN

Review: • Study the words you have missed. Follow the study steps.

Listen: • Do what your teacher tells you to do.

Review: • Take the review trial test. Listen carefully to the sounds in each word. Think what letters stand for them.

            • Look for mistakes before you check your test.

            • Check your test.

Write: • Write the sentences your teacher reads. Listen carefully.

            • Study your words. Follow the study steps.

            • Try Something New.

Review: • Take the review final test.

            • Mark your score on your Progress Chart.

HOW TO MAKE YOUR PROGRESS CHART

- Keep a record of your final tests.
- Make your own Progress Chart.
- Make it like the sample.
- Write the lesson numbers along the bottom.
- On the left side, number down from 0 to 7.
- Mark your chart like the sample.
- Can you make your line go up?

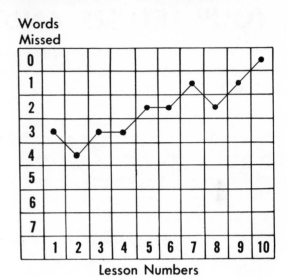

Words Missed

Lesson Numbers

HOW TO MAKE YOUR STUDY LIST

- Make a study list every week.
- Make it like the sample.
- Write the words you find hard.
- Keep the list all week.
- Keep it in your notebook.

Study List

shall
people
world
road

9

HOW TO WRITE
YOUR LETTERS AND NUMERALS

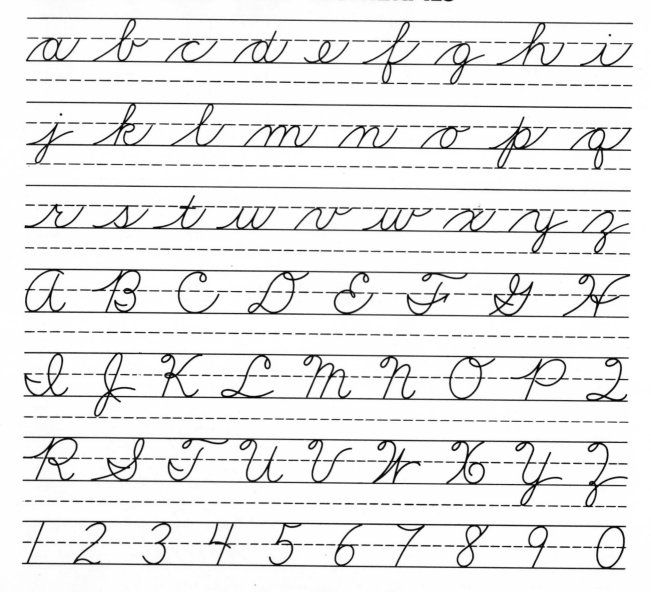

Additional Spelling Words

Lesson					
1	rip	shells	shy	sly	spy
2	bean	farms	peach	slick	tick
3	skates	stir	stormy	stuff	tracks
4	broom	flock	foods	locks	punch
6	blade	brass	fruits	greet	rank
7	bears	bits	drown	pit	trap
8	bone	hopes	lakes	slate	slope
9	daylight	daytime	forenoon	sailboat	workman
11	blowing	flooding	snowsuit	storming	Sundays
12	feeding	heel	paying	peel	needing
13	cooking	beating	nearing	rocks	seating
14	bows	mornings	shiny	tinsel	trim
16	toad	tube	tune	tunes	whale
17	bathtub	mask	masked	task	wheel
18	bills	holds	mold	sigh	sighs
19	blues	colors	mast	mist	yellows
21	bumps	cheeks	cord	mumps	steps
22	batter	batters	bitter	resting	tease
23	playful	roar	sailors	shout	swims
24	chart	dart	lark	floors	parks
26	dine	cakes	lines	mines	winner
27	grant	graph	grim	grind	grip
28	blast	cast	crow	sevens	thirds
29	fare	hare	mare	pare	stare
31	cart	shark	thorn	web	yarn
32	diving	hiding	pleasing	ruling	waving
33	bound	bounce	bait	chew	mount
34	alarm	brace	charm	pace	warn

LESSON 1

try   people

trip   river

shall   world

ship   road

fly

★

sail   port   dock

A Trip

Today we are going to take a
trip.
Shall we fly in an airplane or
sail in a ship?

The ship we might take is tied
at the dock.
See how the waves make it sway
and rock!

All around the world we shall
roam,
To lands and people far from
home.

Many a river and many a
road,
Many a cargo the ship does
unload.

Now we are home and what do
you say,
Shall we try to sail again some
day?

Know About Your Words

a. Write the spelling words that begin like the names of the pictures.

1

2

b. Which two spelling words rhyme with the word this picture makes you think of?

c. Which two spelling words end with **d**?

Understand Your Words

a. Write four spelling words that name things in the picture.

b. Who Am I? Use spelling words.

1. I say, "Buzz, buzz."

2. A car rides over me.

3. Fish live in me.

4. I am a large boat.

5. I am round and I turn.

I am Heather. I will help you spell.

13

LESSON 2

each   once

miss   city

clean   sick

such   farm

sell

————————★————————
ranch   center   village
————————————————

STUDY

STEPS!

City or Farm?

Where do you find it? Write **city** or **farm** for each picture.

1

2

3

4

5

6

14

Know About Your Words

Write the word that does not start with the same letter as the other words in each set.

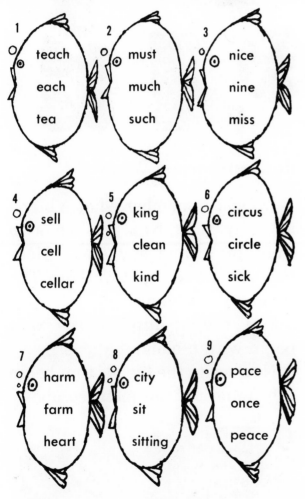

1. teach / each / tea
2. must / much / such
3. nice / nine / miss
4. sell / cell / cellar
5. king / clean / kind
6. circus / circle / sick
7. harm / farm / heart
8. city / sit / sitting
9. pace / once / peace

• Check your trial test.

Understand Your Words

This is a spelling word hunt. See if you can find the right spelling word for each sentence.

1. Tim lives on a _____.
2. He works hard _____ day.
3. He must keep the barn _____.
4. Often Father goes to the city to _____ his animals.
5. _____ in a while Tim goes, too.
6. It is _____ fun!
7. Tim likes the big _____.
8. One day Tim couldn't go because he was _____.
9. "I shall _____ going to the city," he said.

LESSON 3

stay	money
stand	start
land	stop
still	store

bank

★

| frost | clouds | plants |

Remembering Blends

Do you remember what a blend is? Say **top**. Now put an **s** in front of it and say **stop.** Hear how the **s** and **t** go together. The **st** sound is a **blend.**

Say the spelling words that begin with a blend.

Now write the blends that begin the names of the pictures above.

Spelling secret number 1: LISTEN!

Know About Your Words

a. Write six spelling words that begin with the same blend.

b. Write the two spelling words that rhyme.

c. Write the spelling word with a double **l**.

d. Write the spelling word that begins with the same letter as the name of each picture.

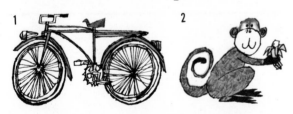

e. People cannot read what we write unless we write neatly. Practice writing each of these letters.

Understand Your Words

Write the name of the picture that does not belong in each row.

17

LESSON 4

room	food	eight
only	o'clock	supper
dinner	table	lunch

---★---

| meat | drink | soup | salad |

What Word?

Complete the sentences.

1. It's _____ o'clock. Sally helps set the _____ for breakfast.

2. Twelve _____. Time for _____.

3. Sally is at school. Mother and Baby are the _____ ones at home.

4. At six _____ it's _____ time.

5. Judy has come to visit. Sally makes _____ for another place at the table.

6. Judy helps bring in the _____.

7. It's _____ o'clock. Bedtime.

18

Know About Your Words

a. Write the spelling words that have double letters.

b. Write a spelling word that rhymes with the name of each picture.

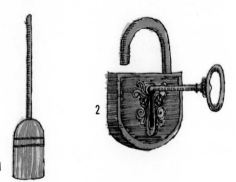

Use Your Dictionary

Put these words in alphabetical order and write them in your dictionary.

food	lunch
only	room
ate	dinner

Understand Your Words

a. Write the names of things missing in the pictures. Each name is a spelling word.

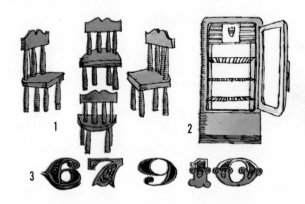

b. Can you write three spelling words that name meals?

c. Which spelling word means **of the clock**?

Remember Your Progress Chart.

19

LESSON 5

Something Old

Review: Study the words that you have missed. Follow the study steps.

1	2	3	4
try	each	stay	room
trip	miss	stand	only
shall	clean	land	dinner
ship	such	still	food
people	once	money	o'clock
river	city	start	table
world	sick	stop	eight
road	farm	store	supper
fly	sell	bank	lunch

Listen: 1. Write the two letters that begin each word your teacher says.

2. Write the two letters that end each word your teacher says.

Write: Write the sentences your teacher reads.

Something New

a. Write the letter that begins the name of each picture.

b. Write the letter that ends the name of each picture.

c. Write the two letters that begin the name of each picture.

Write the two letters that end the name of each picture.

21

LESSON 6

friend   place

grade   thank

should   front

green   grass

children   plant

―――――――★―――――――

fruit   grape   shop

plum   cherry

Make your study list. Use it all week.

Looking for Vowel Clues

Say the name of each picture above. Listen to the **a** sound. Which spelling words have the same **a** sound? This is the **short a** sound.

Study the list of words below. Write the words with the short **a** sound.

grape	**thank**	**grass**
plant	**place**	**grade**

Why is the sound of **a** short in the words you wrote? How many vowels does each short **a** word have?

To help you remember about short vowels in words, finish this sentence: When a word has only one vowel, the vowel is usually ―――――――――――.

Know About Your Words

a. Write the spelling words that begin with the same blends as the names of the pictures.

b. Think of the missing letters and write spelling words.

1. sh _ _ _ d

2. ch _ _ _ _ _ n

3. th _ _ k

Understand Your Words

a. Can you write a spelling word for each sentence?

1. Why is the _____ door open?

2. Those apples are too _____ to eat.

3. Bill is my _____.

4. Next year you will be in the fourth _____.

5. It is good manners to say _____ you.

b.

Use these words to write a sentence about the picture:

are   there   eight   only

in   children   our   grade

The Trap

LESSON 7

water   brown

fat   bear

horse   apple

corn   bit

began   sweet

★
horseback   team   wagon

What can you do to improve in spelling?

Read the story and find the spelling words.

"That bear must be getting fat," Father told Seth. "He steals sweet corn from our fields and visits the apple trees."

That afternoon Seth and Father made a bear trap. They dug a hole and covered it with branches.

The next morning Seth tiptoed to the trap. He began to feel afraid. What if an angry bear had fallen in?

Peeking through the branches, he saw a bit of brown fur and one frightened eye. Then he saw a long, pink ear.

"A rabbit! It's a rabbit!" he cried. "I've got a new pet."

Know About Your Words

a. Listen to the **or** sound as you say **horn**. Write the spelling words that have **or**.

b. Did you know that one letter is silent in double-letter words? Which spelling words have double letters?

c. Which spelling words end with **r**?

d. Can you make rhymes? Use spelling words.

1. My old black cat

   is big and _____.

2. The house in town

   was painted _____.

3. He needed a _____

   to make it fit.

Understand Your Words

a. Think again! Write the name of the picture that does not belong in each row.

b. Write spelling words that mean the opposite of these words.

stopped   **sour**   **thin**

LESSON 8

write	use
hope	ice
close	early
white	lake
upon	late

─────────────★─────────────

Halloween   pumpkin   witch

More Vowel Clues

Say the name of each picture above and listen to the vowel sounds. Which spelling words have the same vowel sounds?

Vowels that say their own names are called **long vowels.** Study the words below and write the ones with long vowels.

hit   hope   use   lap

How are the words you wrote alike? Where do they have an **e**? It is the **e** that tells you the first vowel in the word is long.

To help you remember, finish this sentence:

When a word has two vowels and the last letter is an **e**, the first vowel is usually _____.

Know About Your Words

a. Can you write spelling words with the same vowel sound as the name of each picture?

b. Sometimes **y** is a vowel. Which spelling word ends with **y**?

c. Which spelling word does not end with a vowel?

STOP!
Record your words for review.

Understand Your Words

a. Write spelling words that tell about the pictures.

b. Write a spelling word for each meaning.

1. On.

2. Wish.

3. Opposite of **black.**

4. Shut.

Use Your Dictionary

Words are listed in the dictionary in alphabetical order. Write these words in your dictionary. Write a sentence for each word.

write   hope   use

LESSON 9

things	wants	outside
same	wanted	without
side	upon	afternoon
	birthday	

────────────★────────────

within	outdoors	inside

Building Words

Do you know that you can build words? Just as a mason puts mortar and bricks together to build a wall, you can put words together to build new words.

Try it! Can you put **sail** and **boat** together to make a new word?

Words that are made from two words put together are called **compound words.**

Can you find some **compound words** in your spelling list?

Two things to remember that will help you spell and use compound words are:

1. The spelling of each small word usually stays the same in the compound word.

2. The meanings of the small words help you know the meaning of the compound word.

Know About Your Words

a. Be a word detective. Which spelling word belongs in each shape?

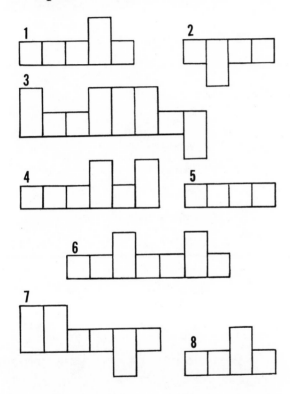

b. Good spellers write neatly! Practice writing these letters.

Understand Your Words

a. Write the spelling words that mean the opposite of:

with   morning   inside

b. Write the correct word to complete each sentence.

1. He _____ more candy.
   (want, wants)

2. His birthday and mine are

   on the _____ day.
   (some, same)

3. She put all the _____
   (thing, things)
   away.

c. Put these words in the right order and write a sentence.

wanted   outside   he   to
     go   afternoon   this

• Did you remember how to begin and end your sentence?

LESSON 10

Something Old

Review: Which words have you missed? Study them. Look at each one carefully before you write it. Follow the study steps.

6	7	8	9
friend	water	write	things
grade	fat	hope	same
should	horse	close	side
green	corn	white	wants
children	began	upon	wanted
place	brown	use	upon
thank	bear	ice	birthday
front	apple	early	outside
grass	bit	lake	without
plant	sweet	late	afternoon

Listen:

Listen to each pair of words your teacher says. Write **S** if they have the same vowel sound and **D** if they have different vowel sounds.

Write: Write the sentences your teacher reads.

Something New

a. Think of the missing vowels and write the names of the pictures.

1. h____t
2. b____d
3. m____n
4. d____g
5. sh____p

6. s____n
7. d____ll
8. dr____ss
9. b____ll
10. ____pple

b. Write the correct word for each sentence.

1. A friend gave _____ the toys.   (us, use)

2. The plane _____ a smooth landing.   (mad, made)

3. She wore a pretty red _____.   (hat, hate)

4. The door was _____ open.   (not, note)

5. Where did you _____ my toys?   (hid, hide)

6. Mother opened a _____ of beans.   (can, cane)

7. We took a _____ on the train.   (rid, ride)

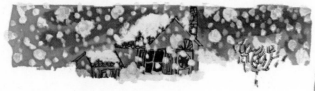

LESSON 11

close	keep	warm
nice	winter	full
open	Sunday	wind
	summer	

――――――★――――――

windy	flood	storm

Summer or Winter?

Write **summer** or **winter** for each sentence.

1. The boys and girls are wearing snowsuits as they walk to school. It is _____ time.

2. A farmer is looking at the corn in his field to see if it is ripe. It is _____ time.

3. Children are building huge sand castles at the beach. It is _____ time.

4. It is five o'clock and the sky is dark. It is _____ time.

5. At school the children are making valentines for their friends. It is _____ time.

Say the second study step.

32

Know About Your Words

a. Listen! Say the words in each row. Write the word that does not have the same vowel sound as the other two.

1. clock   close   clop
2. wise   wire   wind
3. full   fun   fudge
4. kept   keep   kettle
5. wave   way   warm
6. hit   nice   sit

b. Think of the missing letters and write spelling words.

1. _ _ _ _ se   2. _ _ _ ll
3. k_ _ _ _   4. win_ _ _ _
5. s_ _ _ _ _ _   6. win_
7. S_ _ _ _ _ _   8. n_ _ e
9. o_ _ _   10. w_ _ m

c. Write the spelling words with double letters.

Understand Your Words

Can you write spelling words to finish the sentences? Use the pictures to help you.

1. The coffee is _____.

2. The door is _____.

3. The glass is _____.

4. It is his to _____.

5. Today is _____.

33

LESSON 12

tree	trees	feel
need	weeks	pay
week	feed	meet
	days	

★

dew   pair   hour   buy   won

SPELLING PLAN!

Still More Vowel Clues

Say the name of each picture above and listen to the vowel sounds. Did you hear the **e** and **a** say their names? Each word has a long vowel. Which of these words have long vowels?

fed	**met**	**pat**	**feel**
feed	**dad**	**meet**	**fell**

Can you tell why the vowel is long in these words? Are there two vowels together in each word that has a long vowel?

Try to write a sentence to help you remember why these words have long vowels.

34

Know About Your Words

a. Say the words in each row. Write the word that does not have the same vowel sound as the other two.

1. shell   tree   bed
2. feel   bus   truck
3. hand   days   clam
4. cane   skate   meet
5. need   net   next

b. Use your spelling words to make rhymes.

1. A swarm of bees

   was in the _____.

2. When did he say

   he was going to _____?

3. The farmer will _____

   to plant the seed.

4. We played hide-and-seek

   for one whole _____.

Understand Your Words

Take the words out of the box and put them in the right sentences.

1. Sarah will _____ us.
2. Our party is next _____.
3. Gus will _____ the dog.
4. Christmas is in two _____.

Use Your Dictionary

A dictionary tells the meanings of words. In your dictionary write the words that mean:

give   join   touch

Now write a sentence for each word.

LESSON 13

played   looking   eating

looked   walk   talk

playing   near   talking

far

★

swing   recess   climb

Can you say the third study step?

Finding Base Words

How are these words alike?

played   playing

Say the part that is the same. Did you say **play**? **Play** is a base word. We say the base of the word **playing** is **play**. The base of **played** is **play**.

Write the base of each of these words.

1. eating   2. looking

3. talking   4. looked

Know About Your Words

a. Write the word in each group that has a different ending.

1. played   stayed
   rated   playing

2. walk   walking
   cooking looking

3. looking walking
   playing looked

4. walked eating
   talked   played

b. Which spelling words rhyme with **chalk**?

c. Write the spelling words that end with **r**.

Have you made progress in spelling? What can you do to improve?

Understand Your Words

a. Which is it — **far** or **near**?

1. A star.   2. China.

3. The floor. 4. A cloud.

b. Finish the sentences.

1. Joan is _____.
   (talk, talking)

2. A man _____
   (played, playing)
   the horn.

3. He is _____
   (look, looking)
   at the stars.

• Write four words that were hard for you to learn this week.

LESSON 14

Christmas Morning

children	sister	love
child	Christmas	train
brother	morning	aunt
	next	

───────★───────

cousins	uncle	eve

Good spellers write neatly.

Find the spelling words in the story and write four spelling words that are not in the story.

Christmas morning came at last! John had been a very good child all month. Surely Santa must have brought the train he wanted! Happy and excited, John raced downstairs.

His older brother and sister were already at the tree. Such beautiful gifts! But John kept looking for his dream. Finally he saw it. Shiny red and streaked with silver, his train was waiting for him.

Know About Your Words

a. Trim the tree! Think of the missing vowels and write spelling words.

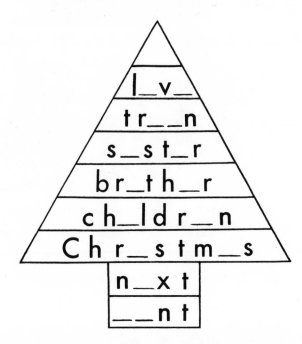

b. Listen to the **er** sound as you say **mother**. Write two spelling words with this sound.

c. Practice these letters.

Understand Your Words

a. Write the spelling words that name kinds of people.

b. Finish each sentence with a spelling word.

1. The early part of the day is the _____.

2. To like very much is to _____.

3. It is my turn _____.

4. There are three _____ in our family.

5. _____ is in December.

PROGRESS CHART!

LESSON 15

Something Old

Review: Study the words you have missed.

11	12	13	14
close	tree	played	children
nice	need	looked	child
open	week	playing	brother
keep	trees	looking	sister
winter	weeks	walk	Christmas
Sunday	feed	near	morning
summer	days	far	next
warm	feel	eating	love
full	pay	talk	train
wind	meet	talking	aunt

Listen: Write the vowel you hear in each word your teacher says.

Write: Write the sentences your teacher reads.

Something New

a. Add these words to the words in the puzzle to make compound words.

    after   **foot**   **in**   **to**   **side**   **birth**

Across

1. Special day.

3. When school is out.

5. Opposite of **inside.**

Down

2. This night.

4. A ball to kick.

6. In + to.

b. What Am I? Use one of the two choices for each answer.

1. I fall from the sky.   (ran or rain)

2. You sleep on me.   (bed or bead)

3. I am a place to sit.   (set or seat)

4. I am a bright color.   (red or read)

5. I am an animal.   (got or goat)

6. I am part of the stairs.   (step or steep)

LESSON 16

when	which	small
what	sure	times
while	took	turn
	large	

———————★———————

wide	tiny	thin

Can you say the fourth study step?

The Lost Goat

Write spelling words to complete the story.

"I wonder _____ Mr. Jones will say _____ he sees the goat in his front yard," said Bob. Bill looked down the street. He wondered about Mr. Jones, too.

"What should we do _____ we wait for Mr. Jones?" asked Bill. "Do you think we should chase the goat away? We could take him home if we knew _____ house was his."

"I don't know what to do," said Bob.

———————————————————————

What do you think happened next? Can you finish the story?

Know About Your Words

Say the word in each fish that does not have the same vowel sound as the other two. Write your answers.

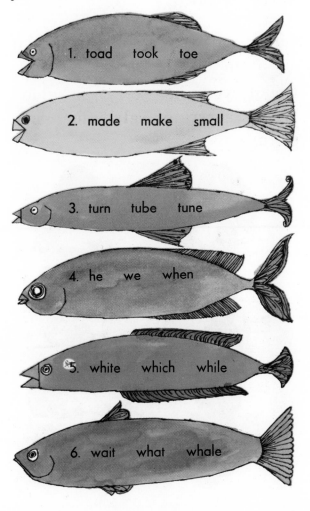

1. toad   took   toe
2. made   make   small
3. turn   tube   tune
4. he   we   when
5. white   which   while
6. wait   what   whale

Understand Your Words

a. Write two spelling words with opposite meanings.

b. Write spelling words with these meanings.

1. Big.
2. Certain.
3. Go around.
4. During.
5. At that time.
6. Carried.
7. Little.
8. More than one time.

Good spellers know how to study.

43

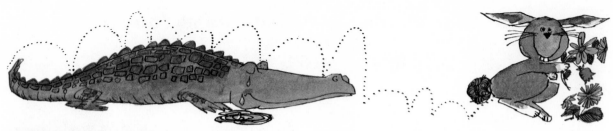

LESSON 17

called   happy

ask   ago

glad   both

asked   sorry

again   sing

———————★———————

song   music   gay

STUDY LIST!

Sorry or Glad?

Look at the pictures. If you were the child in each picture, would you be sorry or glad? Write **sorry** or **glad** for each picture.

Know About Your Words

a. Think of the missing letters and write spelling words.

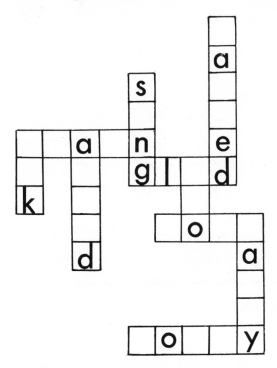

b. Practice these letters.

c. Write the base words.

called　　　**asked**　　　**singing**

Understand Your Words

Write the word that does not belong in each train.

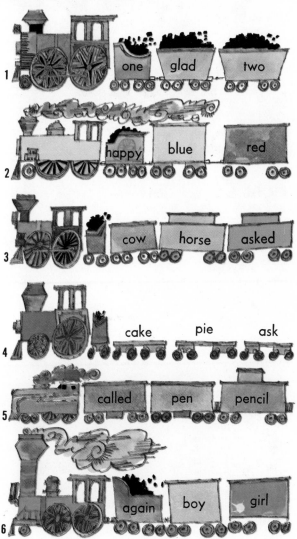

ABCDEFGHIJKL
MNOPQRSTU
VWXYZ

LESSON 18

right	left	hold
bring	lot	carry
high	heard	bill
	life	

★

butter	fish	vegetables

Look for silent letters.

Alphabetical Order

Can you say the ABC's? It is very useful to know the order of the letters in the alphabet. It helps you to find words in a dictionary or names in a telephone book.

Let's see how well you know your ABC's. Write the letter that comes before each of these letters.

__f __t __ x __ r

Write the letter that comes after each of these letters.

d__ j__ l__ q__

Now write these words in alphabetical order.

right   bring   high   left

Know About Your Words

a. Say the name of each picture. Write the spelling words with the same vowel sounds.

 1

 2

b. Write the spelling word with a long **o**.

c. Write the spelling word with a short **o**.

d. Which two spelling words have both **a** and **r**?

Review words!

Understand Your Words

a. Which word does not belong in each row?

1. car	carry	bus
2. high	fast	slow
3. jay	robin	bring
4. hot	lot	cold

b. Is it **left** or **right**? Write the correct word for each picture.

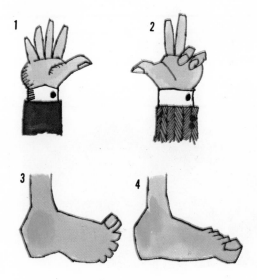

47

LESSON 19

away	always	gold
most	blue	sold
never	than	May
	yellow	

———————★———————

sunshine	sunset	sunburn
sundown		sunny

———————————————————

STUDY

STEPS!

Linda's Letter from Mexico

Find the spelling words in the story.

May 10

Dear Jane,

I like Mexico. I've never been so far away from home. Shopping is the most fun because you always try to buy things at a lower price than they ask.

We bought a Mexican doll with a gold dress.

"Ten pesos," said the lady.

"It's beautiful," said Mother, "but that is too much."

"You are a nice lady," said the storekeeper. "You may have it for nine pesos."

I will write you again soon.

Adios,

Linda

48

Know About Your Words

a. Which spelling words have **ay**?

b. Which spelling words rhyme with **cold**?

c. Write the spelling word that fits in each shape.

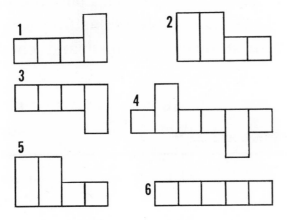

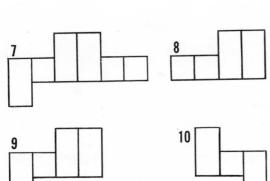

Understand Your Words

a. Do you know your colors? Write a color for each of these:

sun   **sky**

b. Write **always** or **never** for each question.

1. Have you jumped over the moon?

2. Do all bicycles have wheels?

3. Do people need food to live?

4. Do trees talk?

5. Is water wet?

c. Practice these letters.

LESSON 20

Something Old

Review: Study the words that have given you trouble. Look at each one and say it carefully. Look at each letter as you say a word. Write your words on a piece of paper and check yourself.

16	17	18	19
when	called	right	away
what	ask	bring	most
while	glad	high	never
which	asked	left	always
sure	again	lot	blue
took	happy	heard	than
large	ago	life	yellow
small	both	hold	gold
times	sorry	carry	sold
turn	sing	bill	May

Listen: Write the vowel you hear in each word your teacher says.

Write: Write the sentences your teacher reads.

Something New

A Word Zoo

What words belong in each cage? Write your answers.

winter	four	week	colt
three	summer	sheep	children
goat	brother	two	one
sister	horse	child	days

People

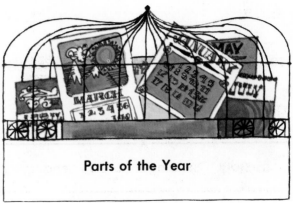

Parts of the Year

Names for Numbers

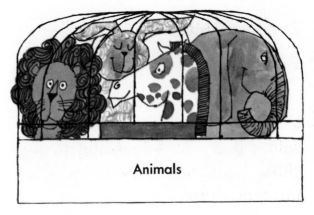

Animals

LESSON 21

alone	sent	sure
end	friend	picture
send	also	almost
along		card

───────────★───────────

friendly   sending   surely   ending

Jimmy's Mumps

Find the spelling words.

Jimmy had the mumps and was tired of staying home alone. He said, "If I sent something to my class, I am sure they would send me something."

He drew a funny picture of himself and sewed two balloons to the paper to show how his cheeks looked. Soon a letter came from his class. This is what it said:

> We send this card to our
>   friend,
> And hope that soon the
>   mumps will end.
> We're sorry you have those
>   horrible lumps,
> Those bumpity, lumpity,
>   humpity mumps.

Can you say the fifth study step?

52

Know About Your Words

a. Can you write spelling words that rhyme with these words?

bend   song   went

hard   pure   bone

b. Write the spelling words that begin with **a.**

c. Think of the missing letters and write spelling words.

  __ l __ ng   __ i __ __ u __ e

  __ lm __ st   s __ r __

  __ a __ __   __ e __ t

  fr __ __ nd   __ e __ d

Look at each letter.

Understand Your Words

a. Write a spelling word for each meaning.

1. Opposite of **begin.**

2. Certain.

3. In addition to.

4. By yourself.

5. Someone you like.

6. A painting or a drawing.

b. Write the correct word for each sentence.

1. I will _____ you a
   (send, sent)

   present.

2. He _____ me a
   (send, sent)

   letter.

3. The letter was _____
   (send, sent)

   by airmail.

LESSON 22

dear	please	Mrs.
because	better	Mr.
letter	Miss	below
best		rest

★

ft.	yd.	Dr.	St.	doz.

Making Words Shorter

Your spelling words **Mr.** and **Mrs.** stand for two longer words. Did you know that these words are **Mister** and **Mistress**?

Sometimes letters are used to take the place of a longer word. These short words are called **abbreviations.** What is at the end of each abbreviation?

Look at the words below. Match each abbreviation with the longer word for which it stands.

Mr.	Doctor
yd.	Street
Dr.	Mister
St.	yard
doz.	dozen

Know About Your Words

Write the spelling word that fits in each shape.

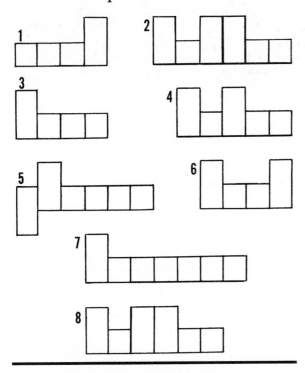

Use Your Dictionary

Put these words in alphabetical order. Then write them in your dictionary.

best **because** **better** **below**

Understand Your Words

a. Write the spelling words that are titles.

b. Which is it — **best** or **better**?

1. Jane likes pie _____ than cake.

2. She likes apple pie _____ of all.

3. Jack is the _____ player in his grade.

c. How well can you write these letters? Practice each one.

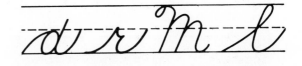

Are you making progress?

55

LESSON 23

above	about	across
behind	around	hurt
before	its	heard
under	hear	brought

★

seashore	mountains	forests

SPELLING PLAN!

Willy the Whale

Find the spelling words.

Have you ever heard about Willy?

Willy is a playful whale who likes to swim around big ships.

Sometimes he puts his head above the water and swims behind them.

Sometimes he goes under them.

Before he dives, Willy blows water with a roar that sailors can hear across the waves. He sounds hurt or angry, but he is just having fun.

Willy is a playful whale.

Know About Your Words

a. Write four spelling words that begin with the same letter.

b. Which spelling words begin with the same letters as the names of the pictures?

1
2

3
4

Can you tell three things good spellers must do?

Understand Your Words

a. Write the spelling words that mean the opposite of the words below.

ahead	after
over	below
left	help

b. Write the word that does not belong in each row.

1.	table	across	chair
2.	about	watch	clock
3.	bus	train	hurt
4.	car	heard	truck
5.	hot	cold	its

LESSON 24

part	wood	eight
rain	year	park
spring	window	month
floor	poor	tonight

---★---

signal   telephone   radio   wires

Listen to vowel sounds.

Linguistic Cousins

Did you know that **moon** and **month** are cousins?

When Young Bear, the Indian boy of long ago, told of things that happened many moons past, this was like saying many months ago.

Sometimes our moon looks like a great silver globe in the sky. At other times it is a smaller globe and not so bright. And sometimes it is only a sliver of light.

The way the moon looks changes each night in a month. When Young Bear saw the bright round full moon in the sky, he knew it would be many days before he would see it again. We now call that period of time one month.

58

Know About Your Words

a. Get out your

Find the spelling words with these letters:

ai   oo   ar   on

b. Unscramble these words and put them in alphabetical order.

c. Think of the missing letters and write spelling words.

w __ nd __ w   p __ __ r

__ __ ght   __ __ __ __ ght

r __ __ n   __ __ __ ing

m __ __ __ h   p __ __ k

__ __ oo __   y __ __ r

Understand Your Words

Write the correct word to complete each sentence.

1. The _____ after
   (mother, month)
   April is May.

2. Every _____ I
   (year, month)
   have a birthday.

3. On the beach an old man
   gathered _____.
   (roof, wood)

4. March is the first month of
   _____.
   (spring, winter)

5. Today it may _____.
   (rain, raw)

6. My room is on the third
   _____.
   (flour, floor)

59

LESSON 25

Something Old

Review: Look carefully at the words you missed. Say each word to yourself. Write your words on a piece of paper and check them carefully. Look at each letter as you check.

21	22	23	24
alone	dear	above	part
end	because	behind	rain
send	letter	before	spring
along	best	under	floor
sent	please	about	wood
friend	better	around	year
also	Miss	its	window
sure	Mrs.	hear	poor
picture	Mr.	across	eight
almost	below	hurt	park
card	rest	heard	month
		brought	tonight

Listen: Are you tuned in? Write the ending of each word your teacher says.

Write: Write the sentences your teacher reads.

Something New

a. What time is it?

one   **four**   **five**   **six**   **seven**   **ten**

b. Write a word that will rhyme, but check your spelling every time.

end	ground	lark	stood
rest	bring	fear	fight
thunder	love	belong	mind

LESSON 26

would	mine	dinner
could	pretty	watch
fine	large	candy
line	o'clock	cake
	party	

★

finest   finer   largest   larger

Write neatly.

Ruth's Birthday

Find the spelling words.

Sally was helping Mother with Ruth's birthday dinner party.

"Hurry, Sally. It's nearly six o'clock. Oh, watch out!"

Too late! Sally slipped. Cake and fine pieces of broken china went everywhere.

"What can we do?" thought Sally. She looked at the candy and colored marshmallows.

"We could use toothpicks to make marshmallow men and put a candle in each one!"

When the guests came, a pretty line of marshmallow men marched across the large table.

Ruth exclaimed, "Everyone has a candle to blow out. Mine is the nicest birthday ever!"

Know About Your Words

a. Write the spelling words that end with a silent **e**.

b. Now write the spelling words that have a silent **l**.

c. Write the spelling word that fits in each shape.

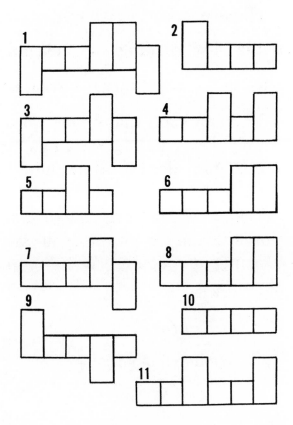

Understand Your Words

a. Which word belongs in each sentence?

fine   **line**   **mine**

1. It is a _____ day today.

2. That book about dogs and cats is _____.

3. My fishing pole has a long _____.

could   **would**

4. I _____ like to go to the zoo.

5. I would go to the zoo tomorrow if I _____.

b. Put these words in the proper order and write two sentences.

1. would I some like cake

2. time is dinner at eight o'clock

63

Words with Endings

Knowing about base words and endings helps you learn to spell many words.

Look at these words. Write each base word.

LESSON 27

does	yours	books
great	brought	reading
paper	teacher	learn
doing	class	word
	yard	

★

classes	learning	teaching
	greatest	

doing	**reading**	**learning**
classes	**teaching**	**greatest**

You can spell many new words simply by adding endings to words you already know how to spell.

Try it. Can you make new words from a word you are learning to spell? Write your answers.

$$\text{learn} + \text{s} = ?$$
$$\text{learn} + \text{ed} = ?$$
$$\text{learn} + \text{ing} = ?$$

STUDY STEPS!

64

Know About Your Words

a. Think of the missing vowels and write spelling words.

y __ rd   b __ __ ks

gr __ __ t   cl __ ss

d __ __ ng   l __ __ rn

r __ __ d __ ng   t __ __ ch __ r

p __ p __ r   w __ rd

d __ __ s   y __ __ rs

b. Write six spelling words that begin with the same letters as things you see in the picture.

Understand Your Words

Complete each sentence with a spelling word.

1. Our _____ wrote six examples on the board.
2. _____ your dog have a name?
3. He enjoyed _____ the book.
4. The whole _____ went on a trip to the farm.
5. I like to _____ about animals at school.
6. He _____ a parrot to the pet show.
7. We have flowers in our _____.
8. Mother was _____ the dishes.
9. Dogs think it is _____ fun to swim.
10. I can spell that _____.
11. He has six _____.
12. Father is reading the _____.

LESSON 28

because	must	began
back	great	grow
first	off	seven
last	few	third
	ground	

────────────★────────────

soil	huge	rear	ahead

Listen for blends.

Choose the Right Word

Use spelling words.

1. The _____ was wet from the rain.

2. Do you ever sing _____ you're happy?

3. Andy jumped _____ the chair.

4. The windows are in the _____ of the room.

5. December is the _____ month of the year.

6. There are only a _____ apples left on the tree.

Know About Your Words

a. Climb down the ladder! Write the word that does not rhyme with the other two on each step.

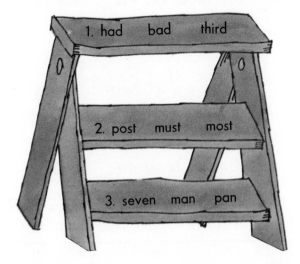

1. had   bad   third
2. post   must   most
3. seven   man   pan

b. Write the spelling words that begin with the same letter as the name of each picture.

1

2

Understand Your Words

a. Write spelling words that have opposite meanings to the words below.

1. last   2. many   3. on

4. front   5. first   6. small

7. ended   8. shrink

b. Which is it?

begun or **began**

1. The movie ―――――――

   three minutes late.

2. The movie has ――――――.

grow or **grown**

3. I hope to ―――――――

   two inches this year.

4. Our new apple tree has

   ―――――――― very big.

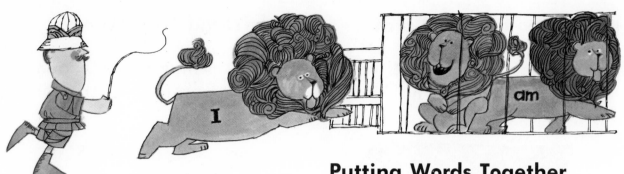

LESSON 29

been   dress

don't   light

I'm   buy

hard   dark

can't   care

street   coat

cannot

★

isn't   aren't   you'll   we've

Putting Words Together

Do you know which spelling words were made from the words below? Try writing them.

do not   cannot   I am

The words you wrote are called **contractions.** The apostrophe (ʾ) shows where letters have been left out.

Now see if you can write the contractions for these words:

you will   we have   are not

Which letters did you leave out in each word?

Do vowels fool you?

68

Know About Your Words

a. Write the spelling words that are contractions.

b. Write four spelling words that have double letters.

c. Feed the sharks! Write a spelling word that rhymes with the word in each shark.

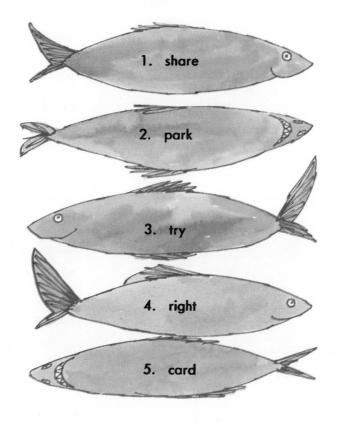

1. share
2. park
3. try
4. right
5. card

Understand Your Words

a. Write the words that are not the names of animals.

goat	coat	care	cow
dog	don't	buy	bat
bear	been	hog	hard

b. Which words are right?

1. The sky was _____.
(dare, dark)

2. Did Father _____
(light, listen)

the bonfire?

3. Yesterday Jane got a

new _____.
(drew, dress)

4. The box felt _____.
(light, bright)

5. On what _____
(street, strong)

do you live?

LESSON 30

Something Old

Review: Study the words you have missed.

26	27	28	29
would	does	because	been
could	great	back	don't
fine	paper	first	I'm
line	doing	last	hard
mine	yours	must	can't
pretty	brought	great	street
large	teacher	off	dress
o'clock	class	few	light
party	yard	ground	buy
dinner	books	began	dark
watch	reading	grow	care
candy	learn	seven	coat
cake	word	third	cannot

Listen: Write the syllable that begins each word your teacher says.

Write: Write the sentences your teacher reads. Write neatly.

Something New

a. Add an Ending! Add an ending to each word below and write a new word.

1. walk   2. look   3. play   4. talk

5. teach   6. eat   7. box   8. week

b. Study each compound word below. Then write the two small words that make each compound word.

1. outside   2. afternoon   3. without   4. birthday

5. inside   6. cannot   7. maybe   8. sidewalk

9. sometime   10. baseball   11. sunshine   12. anytime

c. Write the word that names each picture. Use the words below to help you. You will not use all of the words.

cap	**cot**	**man**	**pants**
cape	**coat**	**mane**	**paints**

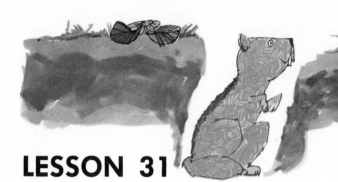

LESSON 31

comes	liked	seen
likes	ate	leave
lives	done	yet
makes	gone	nine
goes		cars

★

sum	report	stories	rules

Chucky Chipmunk

Find the spelling words.

"Will any cars come for a picnic today?" Chucky wondered. He loved picnics.

One of his brothers called, "Here comes a car!" Chucky ran to watch.

"Have you seen any chipmunks yet?" a girl asked. "I want to leave some food." She set nine peanuts on a rock.

"Mother! I see one! He lives in that hole."

Shouting usually makes most chipmunks afraid, but not Chucky. He took a peanut and ate it. When he was done, he stuffed the rest into his cheeks to store in his nest.

Chucky liked picnics because he got food. Summer goes by quickly, but when it is gone he has food for winter.

• Have you made your study list this week?

Know About Your Words

a. Take a good look! Write the spelling word that belongs in each shape.

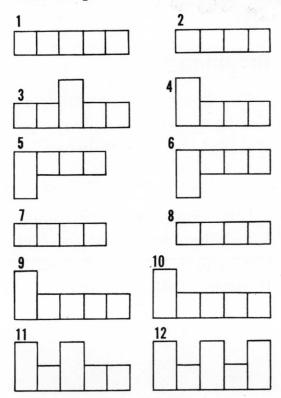

b. Write the six words below in alphabetical order.

yet	**cars**	**liked**
seen	**goes**	**leave**

Understand Your Words

a. Which word belongs in each sentence?

lives or **likes**

1. Joe _____ ice cream.

2. Joe _____ in a

   brick house.

goes or **gone**

3. Joe has _____ home.

4. Joe _____ home each

   day.

b. Put these words in the right order and write a sentence.

he   **nine**   **ate**   **cookies**

c. Practice writing these letters.

LESSON 32

their	making	till
other	small	might
coming	please	catch
another	these	those
having		talking

★

| liking | leaving | living |

Think before you spell.

Dropping the E

You know there are many words that end with a silent **e**. Can you find the silent **e** below?

$$bake + ing = baking$$

But something happened to **bake** when we added the ending. Can you tell what it was? Try it for yourself.

$$live + ing = ?$$

$$skate + ing = ?$$

$$come + ing = ?$$

$$have + ing = ?$$

$$make + ing = ?$$

$$write + ing = ?$$

Know About Your Words

a. Say **this.** Listen to the **th** sound. Write the spelling words with the same **th** sound.

b. Write three spelling words that have base words in which the final **e** was dropped.

c. Write four spelling words to complete the rhymes.

1. The new red ball

   was very _____.

2. He knew it _____

   be too tight.

3. If you _____,

   do not tease.

4. They were _____

   as they went walking.

Look and listen before you spell.

Understand Your Words

Try this puzzle.

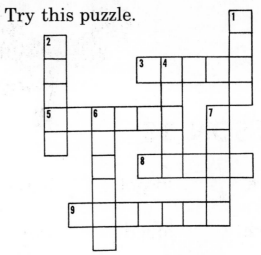

Across

3. Little.

5. Come + ing.

8. Different.

9. An + other.

Down

1. Until.

2. Grab.

4. May.

6. Make + ing.

7. Of them.

LESSON 33

there	forgot	leave
which	found	wait
knew	pair	half
lost	air	hair
forget		fair

★

| chair | sound | pound |
| | stair | mound |

What words do you need to study?

Silly Rhymes

Find the spelling words.

There was an old man from Glare,
Who always got paint in his hair.
  He said, "I have found,
    If I turn round and round,
I tend to forget that it's there."

There once was a little giraffe,
Whose neck was size twelve and
    a half.
  He cried, "I don't care
  If my head's in the air,"
Which made all of his family
    laugh.

There was a lady named Sue,
Who lost the heel of her shoe.
  "I'll leave for the fair
    Where I'll buy a new pair,"
She said, as I knew she would do.

Know About Your Words

a. Think of the missing letters and write spelling words.

1. _ _ _ _ e _ e
2. _ _ o _ _ e _
3. _ _ _ i _ _
4. _ _ o _ _ _ o _

b. Which spelling words rhyme with the words below?

1. cost 2. calf 3. blew

4. bait 5. sound 6. weave

Listening for rhymes helps you to spell.

Understand Your Words

a. Write the word that does not belong in each row.

1. train	bus	which
2. dog	air	cat
3. knew	new	old
4. blue	green	half
5. there	their	your
6. apple	pear	pair

b. Write the missing words.

air **fair** **hair** **pair**

1. The night _____ is cool.

2. The county _____ is coming soon.

3. He bought a _____ of shoes.

4. He combed his _____.

LESSON 34

every	anything	picture
any	something	face
even	everything	foot
ever	nothing	own
head		arm

★

airport	checkroom	scrapbook
	tugboat	timetable

Guess What?

Find the spelling words.

Have you ever heard of an animal six feet long and two feet high, with a head no wider than his neck, and a tongue as long as your arm?

Try to guess what he is.

Almost everything about this animal is strange. His small face has two blind eyes. His mouth isn't anything but a hole at the end of his nose. He hasn't any teeth. His sticky tongue must be busy all day, for he eats almost nothing but insects.

He carries his own umbrella. It is his bushy tail, which he uses every time it rains.

Have you guessed what he is? Turn your book upside-down to see if you were right.

(He is the giant anteater.)

STUDY LIST

78

Know About Your Words

a. When two words are written as one word, they form a compound word. Write the four spelling words that are compound words.

b. Write the four spelling words that begin with the letters **eve**.

c. Write two spelling words that end with silent **e**.

d. Write the name of the picture that does not rhyme with the others in each row.

Understand Your Words

a. Part of each picture is missing. Write what it is.

b. Write the missing part of each compound word.

1. We saw every _____ at the fair.

2. Father asked, "Is there _____ thing we missed?"

3. Tom answered, "There was no _____ we missed."

LESSON 35

Something Old

Review: Study each word you have missed.

31	32	33	34
comes	their	there	every
likes	other	which	any
lives	coming	knew	even
makes	another	lost	ever
goes	having	forget	head
liked	making	forgot	anything
ate	small	found	something
done	please	pair	everything
gone	these	air	nothing
seen	till	leave	picture
leave	might	wait	face
yet	catch	half	foot
nine	those	hair	own
cars	talking	fair	arm

Listen: Write the last syllable of each word your teacher says.

Write: Write the sentences your teacher reads.

Something New

a. Write the contractions for these words.

1. cannot   2. I am   3. are not   4. you will

5. we are   6. do not   7. was not   8. is not

b. Write the abbreviation for each of these words.

Doctor   **Mister**   **Avenue**   **Street**

c. When you write the word with its ending, remember to drop the final **e.**

come + ing = ?   please + ing = ?   live + ing = ?

have + ing = ?   leave + ing = ?   face + ing = ?

make + ing = ?   write + ing = ?   love + ing = ?

take + ing = ?   grade + ing = ?   like + ing = ?

d. Write these words in alphabetical order.

pay   pants   part   past   pack   paid

Something Extra

LESSONS 1-5

a. Write a rhyming word for each of these words.

1. pail	2. brown	3. silk	4. fort	5. cage
6. clock	7. cost	8. pop	9. branch	10. play
11. walk	12. make	13. house	14. came	15. found

b. Use the names below and write the names of the children so they will be in alphabetical order.

Peter   **Connie**   **Stephen**   **Christina**

c. Put these words in the right columns.

Food		Weather		Places	
corn	hail	bank	school	dry	snow
shed	cloudy	windy	cake	ballpark	barn
storm	berries	beans	soup	forest	clams

d. Look at the words above. Make three columns on a big piece of paper. Make three headings for these columns: **b words**, **c words**, and **s words**. In each column write the words beginning with that letter.

e. Can you think of the missing vowels and write words? How are these words alike?

pin__   fin__   bit__   cap__

mat__   spin__   us__   hop__

pan__   rat__   tap__   can__

f. Use a big piece of paper and see how many words you can write by putting other letters in the place of **d** in **dock**.

g. Use a big piece of paper and unscramble these words to write three sentences. Remember capital letters and periods!

1. to store food I buy went to the

2. supper o'clock we eight ate at

3. people there who in live houses on are rivers

h. Can you put these beginnings and endings together and write words? Use a big piece of paper and see how many words you can make. You may use each beginning and ending more than once.

Beginnings

bl	gl
ch	pr
cl	str
dr	sm
fr	

Endings

own	ock	art	ove
ain	eam	all	ink
ow	ag	oke	ank
ack	ue	and	ide
ing	ess		

LESSONS 6-10

a. Say each word carefully. Write the words with long vowel sounds.

grade	car	same
place	side	wants
ice	lake	use
fat	bite	grass
late	plant	than
write	hope	white

b. Write sentences that tell what you do on each of these days.

Halloween   Christmas

Labor Day   Thanksgiving

c. Find the missing letters and write the names of colors.

wh __ te   __ __ ack

__ __ ue   __ __ own

r __ d   or __ __ __ __

d. Find a word in a balloon on the left to go with a word in a balloon on the right and write the compound words you make.

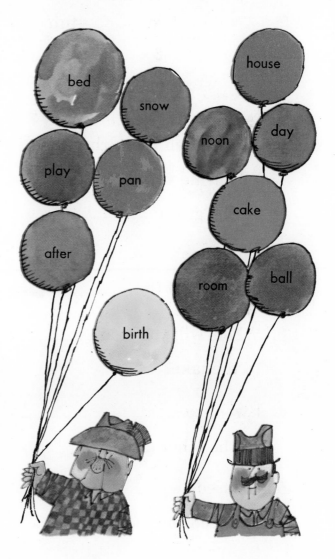

85

e. Put the words in each group in alphabetical order.

1

friend	food	floor
fat	fire	fun

2

bird	blow	began
book	burn	brave

f. Can you finish these rhymes?

1. Whom did you _____

   on the grass?

2. I do hope

   you will cut the _____ .

3. Whom will you _____

   to the lake?

4. I want to _____

   on the other side.

5. He used a _____

   to sweep the room.

g. Put these words in the right order. Remember how to begin and end sentences.

1. trees are there the lake by

2. bear bit the into apple an

3. birthday my is it

h. Have you heard these sayings? See if you can find the right place for each word.

fat	grass	white
sweet	ice	brown

1. as cold as _____

2. as green as _____

3. as _____ as a sheet

4. as _____ as candy

5. as _____ as a berry

6. as _____ as a pig

i. How many words can you write with these beginnings and endings? See how many different combinations you can make.

Beginnings		Endings		
br	sp	own	y	ook
pl	cr	ain	ell	ace
sh	sw	ed	ag	ing
fl	gr	ow	in	eet

j. Who Am I? Write the names of the animals. Use the list below to help you.

tiger	lion	elephant	bear
zebra	monkey	seal	parrot

1. I have black and yellow stripes.

2. I have a long trunk and very thick skin.

3. I can fly and I can talk.

4. I can roar.

5. I am big and furry and sometimes I live in a cave.

6. I live in the water but I am not a fish.

7. I have black and white stripes.

8. I have a long tail and I like bananas.

LESSONS 11-15

a. What's wrong here? Put these compound words together the right way.

afterday   birthnoon

milkyard   barnman

sidecake   panwalk

b. Can you add an ending to each of these words and write a new word?

talk	open
keep	need
feel	pay
meet	warm
plant	keep
friend	feed
play	near
storm	witch
swing	climb

c. A **homonym** is a word that is pronounced like another word, but it is spelled differently and it has a different meaning. **To** and **two** are homonyms. Write a homonym for each word below.

sea	hour	ate
blew	son	whole
meet	know	weak
deer	buy	won

d. Use the homonyms above to help you finish the sentences.

1. I can ＿＿＿＿＿＿＿ you.

2. A ship went to ＿＿＿＿＿.

3. I would like to ＿＿＿＿＿ a new bike.

4. This story is ＿＿＿＿＿ Jimmy.

88

e. Take a letter away from each word below and write a new word.

aunt   nice   open

warm   wind   feed

f. Now add a letter to each word below and write a new word.

pay   ran   tank

ear   net   rain

g. Think of the missing letters and write words.

str __ __ t   str __ p

str __ p   str __ __ m

str __ p __   str __ ng __

str __ ng   str __ __ n

str __ w   str __ y

str __ k __   str __ k __

h. Write the base words.

talking   tallest   played

helps   keeping   higher

i. Can you put these base words and endings together and write three new words?

j. Have you ever helped the librarian? How would you arrange these books to put them on the shelf in alphabetical order? Write the titles in alphabetical order.

Pinto's Journey

Country Train

Children of the Sea

Petunia

89

k. Who Am I? Use the words below to help you write your answers.

monkey	octopus	elephant	giraffe	lion
deer	bull	chicken	calf	turkey

1. I have eight arms and I live in the sea.
2. I am a baby cow.
3. I am a bird you eat on Thanksgiving Day.
4. I have horns and sometimes I wear a ring in my nose.
5. I have a mane and I am called king of beasts.
6. I give you eggs.
7. I have a very long neck.
8. I live in the jungle and I swing through the trees.
9. I am very large and I have tusks.
10. I live in the woods and I am very swift.

l. Say the words below. Write the ones with long vowels.

sail	dock	ranch	town	meat
grape	plum	team	wagon	witch
swing	climb	cousins	uncle	ever
wind	flood	storm	are	buy
swim	clam	eve	calf	deer

LESSONS 16-20

a. Write each of these words in the right column.

Furniture	Food	Buildings

house	cake	table	store	desk	chair
lamp	shed	bread	garage	fish	butter
sofa	ice cream	bank	chest	church	candy

b. Follow the picture clues to write compound words.

c. Can you think of three words to tell how this child feels?

d. Which is it?

hour or **our**

1. This is _____ house.

2. It took an _____ to do it.

ate or **eight**

3. I _____ a banana.

4. It is _____ o'clock.

blew or **blue**

5. The wind _____.

6. Her dress is _____.

e. See how many of these word endings you can use with **keep** and **want**.

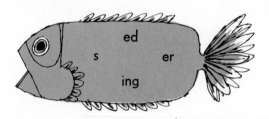

f. Which is it?

whole or **hole**

1. A rabbit lives in a _____.

2. He ate a _____ cake.

know or **·no**

3. Do you _____ John?

4. _____, I do not.

knew or **new**

5. He has a _____ book.

6. I _____ it was true!

son or **sun**

7. He is my _____.

8. The _____ was shining.

g. Who Am I? Use the words below to answer the clues.

cake   house   shed   table   store   desk

butter   lamp   fish   garage   bread   chair

sofa   ice cream   cupboard

1. I live on a street and you live in me.

2. I am here for your birthday.

3. You put food and dishes on me and you sit at me.

4. I am a place to buy things.

5. You work at me and you write on me.

6. You sit on me.

7. I give you light.

8. You keep your tools in me.

9. I am something you eat with butter and jam.

10. You keep your car in me.

11. You can eat me if you can catch me.

12. You put me on your bread.

13. You put me in a soda or in a sundae.

14. I was empty when Old Mother Hubbard saw me.

15. I am big and long and you sit on me.

LESSONS 21-25

a. What is the title of your spelling book? Can you write a title for each of these pictures?

b. Use the words below to complete the sentences. You will not need to use all of the words.

dark	inches	deep
minus	plus	two
feet	dime	ten

1. John is five _____ tall.

2. My hand is three _____ wide.

3. The well is twenty feet _____.

4. A _____ is worth ten cents.

5. Three_____ two is five.

6. Eight _____ two is ten.

c. How many words can you write that rhyme with **sing** and **top**?

d. Can you find a shorter way? Write the abbreviation for each of these words.

1. dozen   2. gallon

3. yard   4. pound

5. quart   6. week

7. year   8. hour

e. Can you write the contractions for these words?

1. was not   2. have not

3. she will   4. has not

5. they are   6. were not

7. I have   8. it is

9. you are   10. did not

f. Add a word to each word below and write compound words.

1. snow   2. base

3. sun   4. any

5. some   6. fire

g. Write words that mean the opposite of the words below.

1. first   2. bottom

3. small   4. never

5. over   6. front

7. stop   8. buy

9. can't   10. far

11. hard   12. short

h. Which is it?

be   or   **bee**

1. Will you _____ here?

2. There is a _____ near the flower.

won   or   **one**

3. There is only _____ left.

4. They _____ the game.

their   or   **there**

5. _____ is one left.

6. It is _____ turn.

i. Run and **jump** are action words. Write action words to finish the sentences below. Use the list of words to help you.

run	jump	hop	pull	laugh	cry
stand	sit	swing	walk	talk	roll

1. The rabbit began to _____ across our front yard.

2. The little boy was so excited he could not _____ still.

3. The parrot was learning how to _____.

4. Children often like to _____ in the snow.

5. The soldiers had to _____ at attention.

6. The story was so funny it made him _____.

7. They had a race to see who could _____ the fastest.

8. The baby was very hungry and began to _____.

9. When the baby was one, he learned to _____.

10. Monkeys like to _____ from trees.

11. He was so happy he began to _____ up and down.

12. He had to _____ a long rope to make the bell ring.

j. Can you add a letter to each word below to write a new word?

got	ton	shut	part	back
thin	mat	were	bat	sip

LESSONS 26-30

a. A **homonym** is a word that is pronounced exactly like another word, but it is often spelled differently and it has a different meaning. Can you write a homonym for the name of each picture below?

b. How many words can you write to rhyme with the words below?

     meat   **flame**   **book**   **slow**

c. Mr. Jones wants to put the vegetables in his market on the shelves in alphabetical order. Can you help him? Write the names of these vegetables in alphabetical order.

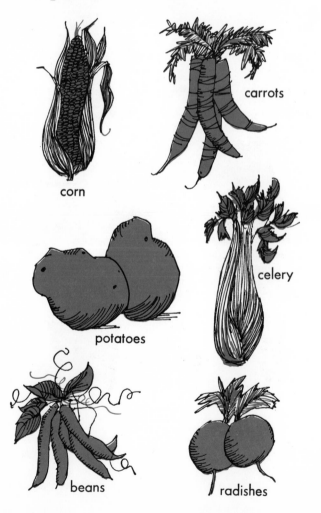

corn

carrots

potatoes

celery

beans

radishes

d. Unscramble each group of letters to write words.

ressd   dogin   inem
tmus   thrid   sslac

e. Complete the sentences with some of the words below.

arm   face   top   legs

nap   switch   pane

1. A desk has a _____ but cannot spin it.

2. A chair has an _____ but cannot raise it.

3. A rug has a _____ but gets no rest.

4. A clock has a _____ but cannot smile.

5. A table has _____ but cannot move.

f. Word arithmetic! Can you do the following examples?

watch + ing = ?   greater − er = ?

do + es = ?   grounded − ed = ?

great + est = ?   grown − n = ?

class + es = ?   seventh − th = ?

read + ing = ?   hardly − ly = ?

g. Finish these sentences with the following words.

seashore   mountains   forests   largest   signal

telephone   radio   wires   larger

1. Our house has many _____ for electricity.

2. In the West there are many _____.

3. I like to talk on the _____.

4. We play in the sand by the _____.

5. There are many trees in our _____.

6. The policeman had to _____ for him to stop.

7. New York is one of the _____ cities in the world.

8. New York is _____ than Boston.

9. We often listen to the news report on the _____.

LESSONS 31-35

a. What does **fair** mean in each of these sentences?

1. We went to the **fair**.

2. The weather is **fair**.

Many words have more than one meaning. On a piece of paper, write two sentences for each word below. Make each sentence show a different meaning.

right	plant
park	part
ship	trip
saw	store

b. What is wrong with these sentences? Can you write them correctly?

1. My father is mr allen.

2. I was born in june.

3. We hunt for eggs on easter.

c. Finish these word towers. See how the first one is done.

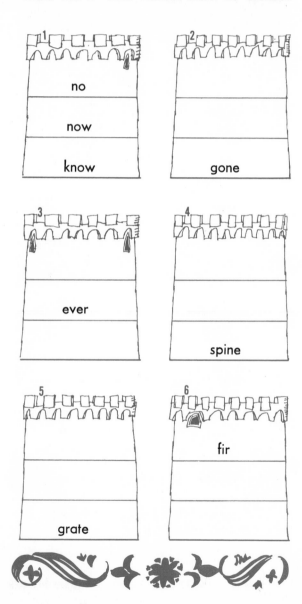

100

d. Can you think of six things to write under each heading? Use a dictionary if you are not sure how to spell a word.

Clothing   **Months**   **Sports**

e. What is missing in each picture? Write your answers.

f. Add **ing** to each word below and write the new words you make.

know   face   hear   race   leave   spend

shine   wire   mine   make   come   live

g. Who Am I? Use the words below to answer the clues.

rules   story   chair   report   timetable   sound

pound   mound   checkroom   airport   scrapbook   tugboat

1. You put pictures in me.

2. I help you to know how much you weigh.

3. You sit on me.

4. You like to tell me and you like to hear me.

5. Airplanes use me.

6. You follow me.

7. In baseball, a pitcher stands on me.

8. You make me when you talk.

9. You give me at school.

10. When you go to a restaurant, you put your coat in me.

11. I tell you when trains arrive.

12. I help big ships go up a river.

How to Use Your Dictionary

This is your dictionary.

We use a dictionary to find out what words mean and how they are spelled.

Words are always listed in the dictionary in **A B C** or **alphabetical** order.

Look at the top of page 106. The two letters at the top of the page tell you what words you can find on that page. You can find words that begin with **k, l, m, n, o,** and **p** on page 106. Is **key** on that page? Is **yarn** on that page?

You will be using your dictionary this year. Your spelling lessons will tell you what to do.

How to Make Your Own Dictionary

You can make your own dictionary to use during the year. You can put words that are hard for you to spell in your dictionary.

Use your notebook. Make sure you put letters at the top of each page so you will be able to write your words in alphabetical order.

When you write words in your dictionary, try to draw a picture for each word and try to write a sentence for each word.

Make your own dictionary look like the dictionary in the back of the book.

Aa

Dd

Picture Dictionary

We count on an **abacus.** We **add** and subtract.

There is a **bear** in the zoo. He is very **big.**

Bring some **cake,** too. Bring a **cup** of tea.

The **deer** likes to run. He **does** it very well.

Ee

He has big **ears.**   The **elephant** is large.

He turned on the **faucet.** Water **flowed** out.

The **gate** is open. **George** opened it.

It is **her** own horn.   She can play the **horn.**

I like them.   There are **icicles** on the trees.

Water is in the **jug.** There is **just** a little.

Kk

Pp

He has a **key**. Do you **know** where it is?

I **like** to hear him roar.   The **lion** is fierce.

I **might** climb it.   The **mountain** is high.

He has a fish in his **net**. The fish is **not** happy.

The **octopus** is big. He looks quite **odd.**

Penguins like ice. They live at the South **Pole.**

Qq

I have a **quarter.** I can spend it **quickly.**

Then he **ran** away. The **rooster** crowed.

He used a **saw.** He cut **several** boards.

This one is **thirty.** Some **turtles** are old.

We have an **umbrella.** It keeps **us** dry.

He was **very** good. The man played his **violin.**

Ww

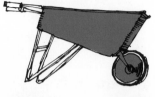

I have a **wheelbarrow.** It has one **wheel.**

My doctor has an **X-ray** machine.

A sweater is made of **yarn.** Do **you** have one?

Zz

A **zebra** is wild. I saw one in the **zoo.**

Your Most Used Spelling Words

about	coming	heard	only	than
again	could	high	other	their
along	days	hope	people	there
also	dear	its	place	these
always	dinner	large	please	things
another	done	last	pretty	took
any	don't	left	right	under
around	ever	letter	room	upon
asked	every	looked	same	use
away	few	lot	sent	wanted
back	fine	love	should	water
because	first	making	side	week
been	found	morning	sister	what
before	friend	most	small	when
better	glad	must	something	which
bring	grade	never	stay	while
brother	great	next	still	white
called	happy	nice	summer	would
children	hard	off	sure	write
close	having	once	teacher	year